W9-AMT-385

RIVER OR THE SOUND

New York Landmarks

A Collection of Architectural and Historical Details

Photography & Text by
Charles J. Ziga

DOVETAIL
BOOKS

"Give me your tired, your poor,
Your huddled masses yearning to breathe free,
The wretched refuse of your teeming shore.
Send these, the homeless, tempest-tost to me,
I lift my lamp beside the golden door!"

From
"THE NEW COLOSSUS"
EMMA LAZARUS, 1883

For Annie

New York Landmarks

Contents

CITY HALL

New York's architectural treasure

CITY HALL PARK, BETWEEN BROADWAY AND PARK ROW

City Hall, completed in 1811, continues to house the Mayor's office and City Council Chambers. It is New York's welcoming center for important dignitaries, returning soldiers, celebrities and athletes. This elegant scaled-down palace combines the *Georgian-Federal* style with *French Renaissance* details. The building is situated in City Hall Park, the town green of the city. Since colonial times, the park has been the site of parades, protests, riots and celebrations.

Joseph F. Mangin and **John McComb,** *Architects.* Awarded the commission by their competition-winning design. McComb is attributed with the *Georgian* style interior and Mangin, a French émigré, with the elegant *French Renaissance* details and graceful ornamentation of the exterior.

The symmetrical two-story building features a one-story central portico and projecting wings. The façade's rows of arched windows are decorated with Corinthian pilasters to each side and swags above. The building was originally finished in white marble with base and north façade of New Jersey brownstone. One hundred and ninety years ago City Hall was at the northern edge of New York City, and therefore the northern side was clad in brownstone in order to save money. By 1895, the building had fallen into terrible disrepair and was threatened by demolition. Because of public outcry, renovations have since occurred. In 1956, the marble exterior, including the north side, was refinished in Alabama limestone. The clock in the cupola was added in 1831 and was the first illuminated clock in New York City. A figure of *Justice*, designed by John Dixey, crowns the cupola.

The interior is classic *Georgian*. At the central rotunda (inset) are a sweeping pair of self-supporting marble stairs. On the second floor of the rotunda, 10 Corinthian columns support a coffered dome with a glass oculus.

N.Y.C. Landmark February 1, 1966.

Schermerhorn Row

Street of ships

FULTON STREET, AT THE SOUTH STREET SEAPORT

Built between 1811 and 1812, in the *Georgian-Federal* tradition of architecture, Schermerhorn Row was one of the earliest commercial developments in New York City. When the area was a major shipping center, its 12 buildings housed chandleries (selling provisions for ships), sail lofts, rope lofts and naval store warehouses.

Peter Schermerhorn, *Merchant and Ship Owner.* Constructed these buildings to lease to sailing merchants. Schermerhorn operated his own prosperous ship chandlery from 243 Water Street.

The four-story row houses on Fulton Street, Front Street and South Street were built on land-filled water lots (land between extremes of high and low tides). Red Flemish bond brickwork, plain stone lintels, arched entrances of brownstone, tall brick chimneys and steep *Georgian* hip roofs of slate are the buildings' original features. The area became a busy commercial district in 1816, when the Brooklyn Ferry put a landing at Schermerhorn's wharf. Soon after, the Fulton Market opened across the street. In the late 1800s dormers and *Greek Revival*-style cast iron storefronts were added to the building to serve ships' passengers. In 1868, the building on the corner of South and Fulton Streets was converted into a hotel. The fifth story and the mansard roof with dormers were added for additional rooms.

In 1968, Schermerhorn Row was protected by the New York City Landmarks Commission and became an integral part of the South Street Seaport Historical District. It was restored in 1983 by **Jan Hird Pokorny** and **Cabrera & Barricklo**, *Architects.*

N.Y.C. Landmark October 29, 1968.

FEDERAL HALL NATIONAL MEMORIAL

Site of the first capitol of the United States
28 WALL STREET

Federal Hall National Memorial is situated on one of New York's most historic sites. Here once stood New York City's first City Hall (later called Federal Hall) where the first U.S. Congress met and where George Washington took his oath as the first president of the United States in 1789. In 1812, the original building was demolished and sold as salvage for $425. The current building, constructed between 1834 and 1842, was originally a U.S. Custom House. It later became a U.S. Sub-Treasury and, in 1939, was listed as a National Monument under the National Parks Service. Today, it serves as a museum for American and New York history.

Ithiel Town and **Alexander Jackson Davis,** *Architects.* Awarded the commission based on their *Greek Revival* design.

Samuel Thompson, *Construction Architect.* **John Frazee,** *Interior Architect.*

The ideals of Greek democracy and Roman republicanism that influenced the Founding Fathers were reflected in their choice of classical architecture for public buildings. This classic Greek temple rests on a high plinth with a steep flight of steps. A portico with 32-foot-high Doric columns supports a simple pediment without ornamentation.

The interior rotunda (inset) is dominated by a paneled dome (not a typical Greek form) that is 60 feet in diameter and which is supported by 16 two-story-high Corinthian columns. The rich, ornate Roman interior contrasts with the simple Greek exterior.

The statue of *George Washington* is by J.Q.A. Ward, 1883.

National Landmark 1939. N.Y.C. Landmark December 21, 1965.

TRINITY CHURCH AND CHURCHYARD

A green oasis amid the concrete
BROADWAY AT WALL STREET

Completed in 1846, after seven years of construction, Trinity Church served the first Episcopalian parish in New York City and was the tallest building in the area until the late 1860s.

Richard Upjohn, *Architect.* English-American. Founder of the American Institute of Architects and its first president, 1857–76.

Richard Morris Hunt, *Architect.* Designed the six sculptured bronze doors illustrating biblical scenes and the history of Trinity Church. The bas-relief detail (inset) represents Revelation VI, verses 15, 16 and 17. Like Upjohn, Hunt was a founder of the American Institute of Architects.

The *Gothic Revival* church, 79 feet wide and 166 feet long, is built of New Jersey brownstone and has flying buttresses, stained-glass windows, Gothic tracery and medieval sculptures. Located at the head of Wall Street, the central tower with octagonal spire measures 280 ½ feet tall. Its bells were imported from London in 1797 and are the oldest in New York. Trinity Church is the third church to be built on the site. King William III of England gave the land to the church in 1697, and the original church, completed a year later, was burned in the Great Fire of 1776. The second church was demolished in 1839 after structural failure.

Trinity Churchyard, established even before the first church (the oldest gravestone dates from 1681), includes graves and memorials of historical New Yorkers such as Francis Lewis (signer of the Declaration of Independence), Alexander Hamilton (Secretary of the U.S. Treasury), William Bradford (founder of the city's first newspaper, the *Gazette*) and Robert Fulton (inventor). It remains one of the last green sites in the Financial District.

N.Y.C. Landmark August 16, 1966.

BROOKLYN BRIDGE

World's first steel-wire suspension bridge

MANHATTAN (CITY HALL PARK) TO BROOKLYN (CADMAN PLAZA)

On May 24, 1883, after 14 years of construction, the Brooklyn Bridge became the first bridge to span the East River, uniting the boroughs of Brooklyn and Manhattan. The bridge's construction cost was over $16 million. It remained the largest bridge in the world until 1903, when Virginia's Williamsburg Bridge (4½ feet longer) was completed.

John A. Roebling, *Engineer.* An immigrant from Prussia and original designer of the bridge. While directing the bridge's surveying, he was injured in an accident and died before construction began.

Colonel Washington A. Roebling. Became the *Chief Construction Engineer* after his father's death.

With its two *Gothic* towers (inset) rising 276 feet, the bridge was the second highest structure in New York in 1883. Only the spire of Trinity Church was taller. Its four main cables made of steel-wires were a first in bridge construction. Each cable, 15¾ inches in diameter, contains 5,434 wires and is 3,515 feet long. The bridge stretches 5,989 feet long overall, with a center span of 1,595 feet between its two towers, and is 85 feet wide.

A grand celebration with fireworks opened the bridge in 1883. One week later, twelve pedestrians were trampled to death on the bridge's promenade when the crowd thought the bridge was collapsing and panicked.

The Brooklyn Bridge has been a source of inspiration to many U.S. artists, including Walt Whitman, Hart Crane, Thomas Wolfe, John Marin and Joseph Stella. The bridge's 100th birthday was celebrated in 1983.

N.Y.C. Landmark August 24, 1967.

Saint Patrick's Cathedral

Dedicated to the patron saint of Ireland

Fifth Avenue, between 50th and 51st Streets

Saint Patrick's is the largest Roman Catholic church in the U. S. and the seat of the Archdiocese of New York. The cathedral took 21 years to build: four times longer and at twice the cost estimated. Cardinal John McCloskey formally blessed and opened the cathedral on May 25, 1879. The spires were completed nine years later, and the Lady Chapel was added in 1906.

Archbishop John Hughes, *First Catholic Archbishop of New York.* Irish immigrant. Announced his plan for Saint Patrick's as a church "worthy of God…and an honor to this great city" in 1850.

James Renwick, Jr., *Architect.* Renwick also designed the original Smithsonian Institution building, "the Castle," in Washington, D. C.

Originally the land was intended for a burial ground, but it was too rocky. When the cathedral was constructed, it stood on the very outskirts of the city, and its spires dominated the surrounding skyline until the 1930s. Today, it is dwarfed by the glass and steel skyscrapers of midtown Manhattan.

The *French Gothic* cathedral, 174 feet wide and 332 feet long, is the eleventh largest church in the world. Constructed of white marble, it is in the shape of a Latin cross with traditional east-west orientation. Above the central entrance is a circular rose window, 26 feet in diameter, flanked by foliated tracery spires 330 feet high. The north tower holds the cathedral's chimes of 19 bells. Three sets of bronze doors adorned with statues of the saints of New York, designed by Charles Maginnis and John Angel in 1949, comprise the cathedral's formal entrances. The bas-relief detail from the central doors (inset) represents Elizabeth Ann Seton, the first American-born saint.

The nave (central seating area) is 108 feet high and 48 feet wide. Forming the cathedral's focal point is the sanctuary, with its 57-foot-high bronze baldachin.

N.Y.C. Landmark October 19, 1966.

Dakota Apartments

It might as well be in the Dakota Territory

72ND STREET AND CENTRAL PARK WEST

The city's first luxury apartment house was named for the remote northwestern Indian territory because it was located so far from the city's center. At the time of its completion in 1884, the building was surrounded by vacant land and squatters' shacks. Early Dakota residents had views of Central Park (still incomplete), Long Island Sound, the undeveloped hills of Brooklyn and the Hudson River.

Edward S. Clark, *Singer Sewing Machine Heir, Developer.* He turned public mockery of his building's location to good account in both name and decoration. Western ornamentations of arrowheads, sheaves of wheat and an Indian head relief (inset) are incorporated into the design.

Henry J. Hardenberg, *Architect.* Also designer of the Plaza Hotel.

Reminiscent of a château, the eight-story yellow brick mass is articulated by brownstone and terra-cotta gables, bay windows, recessed and projecting balconies, cornices, trim and ornamentation. The steeply pitched slate roof is adorned with chimneys, dormers and copper cresting. Surrounding the *German-Renaissance* building is a stylized "moat" with sea monsters and masks of Zeus.

The main entrance, a two-story arched gateway on 72nd Street, leads into an inner courtyard with two fountains. At each of the courtyard's four corners is an entrance and elevator. There were originally 85 apartments, each with 4–5 rooms (a typical living room measures 25 ft. x 40 ft.) with 12- to 15-foot-high ceilings and wood-burning fireplaces. The interiors were finished in mahogany and oak with marble mantels and brass fixtures. Walls 2 feet thick and 18-inch-thick floors make this one of the quietest buildings in the city.

Famous tenants of the Dakota, past and present, include: Boris Karloff, Lauren Bacall, Leonard Bernstein, Roberta Flack and John Lennon.

N.Y.C. Landmark February 11, 1969.

STATUE OF LIBERTY
Liberty Enlightening the World
LIBERTY ISLAND (BEDLOE'S ISLAND), NEW YORK HARBOR

France presented the statue on July 4, 1885, as a gift from the French to the American people. It took 10 years to build at a cost of $400,000. It was dedicated on Bedloe's Island (now Liberty Island) on October 28, 1886.

Édouard-René Lefebvre de Laboulaye, *French Historian.* Paris. Credited with the idea of a statue symbolizing the union of France and the United States in the quest for liberty and freedom.

Frédéric-Auguste Bartholdi, *Sculptor.* Paris. The image was modeled after his mother and Delacroix's painting *Liberty Leading the People to the Barricades.*

Alexandre-Gustave Eiffel, *Engineer.* Paris. Engineered the statue's skeletal frame of iron and steel. He also designed the Eiffel Tower.

Richard Morris Hunt, *Architect.* Designed the statue's 151-foot-high pedestal of Stony Creek granite and concrete. The funds for the pedestal were raised in the United States by public subscription.

The statue, which stands 302 feet tall (with pedestal), is made of 300 copper sheets molded and riveted to and supported by the steel and iron framework. Its crown can accommodate up to 30 people. The length of the upraised arm with torch is 45 feet. Copper oxidizing gives the statue its green color (patina).

Broken shackles at Liberty's feet signify escape from tyranny; the 21-foot-tall torch symbolizes truth and justice illuminating the world; the spikes of her crown denote the seven seas and seven continents; and the tablet (inset) bears the date of the Declaration of Independence: July 4, 1776. After renovation by *architects* **Richard S. Hayden and Thierry W. Despont** (1984–86), she was rededicated on October 28, 1986, for her 100th birthday.

National Monument 1924. N.Y.C. Landmark September 14, 1976.

CENTRAL PARK

New York's emerald treasure

59TH STREET TO 110TH STREET, FIFTH AVENUE TO EIGHTH AVENUE

Central Park, the first planned public park in the United States, is one of New York's, indeed the country's, finest treasures. Since 1857, the park has continued to evolve, meeting the changing needs of society, yet adhering to Olmsted's and Vaux's original design intent.

William Cullen Bryant, *Editor of the* N.Y. Evening Post, and **Andrew Jackson Downing,** *Landscape Architect and Publisher of the* Horticulturist, were instrumental in gathering support for a large public park in New York City.

Frederick Law Olmsted, *Engineer and Landscape Architect,* and **Calvert Vaux,** *Architect.* Won the competition and the $2,000 award with their **Greensward Plan.** Their design integrated architecture with landscaping to accommodate the uneven topography.

The 843-acre park, 2 ½ miles long and ½ mile wide, is located in the heart of Manhattan Island. The park's southern half is more pastoral, with an open landscape, and its northern half is more rugged and wooded. Foot paths, bridal paths, curved carriage drives (to discourage carriage racing) and four sunken transverse roads provided for pedestrian and motor traffic. The 36 arched bridges that grace the park were all designed by Calvert Vaux, and each is different. During construction, over 4 million trees (632 species) and 815 varieties of vines, shrubs and flowers were planted; 10 million cartloads of earth were moved.

The park's major points of interest are the Bethesda Fountain and Terrace (inset), Belvedere Castle, the Mall, Delacorte Theater, Strawberry Fields, Wollman Memorial Rink, the Conservatory Garden and the Zoo.

National Historic Landmark 1935. N.Y.C. Scenic Landmark April 16, 1974.

CARNEGIE HALL

How do you get to Carnegie Hall? — Practice, practice, practice.

57TH STREET AND SEVENTH AVENUE

Carnegie Hall (formerly Music Hall) opened on May 5, 1891, with the American premiere of Peter Ilyich Tchaikovsky conducting his *Marche Solennelle*. Since then, it has become a world-renowned concert hall, more famous for its near perfect acoustics than for its architecture.

Andrew Carnegie, *Steel Magnate, Philanthropist.* A Scottish immigrant, he donated $2 million to build the concert hall at the urging of **Walter Damrosch,** Conductor of the Oratorio Society of New York and the New York Symphony Society.

William Burnet Tuthill, *Architect.* His research of European concert halls and the technology available 100 years ago resulted in the outstanding acoustics of Carnegie Hall.

The hall has been host to the world's greatest conductors, musicians and performers including Toscanini, Bernstein, Ella Fitzgerald, Charlie Parker, the Rolling Stones and the Beatles. In addition, it has served as a lecture hall for such notables as Martin Luther King, Jr., Winston Churchill, Eleanor Roosevelt and Mark Twain. In 1959, Isaac Stern, violinist, rallied support to save Carnegie Hall from demolition.

The famous acoustics are attributed to the soft curved planes of the balconies and the elliptical ceiling, which allows sound to be diffused throughout the 2,804-seat auditorium. The velvet drapery adorning the hall helps to absorb both reverberation and echoes.

The modest exterior is of pale brown Roman brick with Roman arches, pilasters, and terra-cotta ornamentation (inset). The original mansard roof was replaced by a sixth floor of studios, but the tower was retained. Carnegie Hall is an early example of a mixed-use building with offices, studios, shops, a theater, a recital hall and a concert hall.

National Historic Landmark 1964. N.Y.C. Landmark June 20, 1967.

WASHINGTON MEMORIAL ARCH

Exitus acta probat (The end justifies the deed)
WASHINGTON SQUARE NORTH AT FIFTH AVENUE

In 1889, a temporary wood and stucco arch was built to commemorate the centennial anniversary of the inauguration of George Washington as the first president of the United States. Building began on the current memorial arch in 1892, and it was dedicated on April 30, 1895.

William Rhinelander Stewart. Credited with the arch's concept and for raising the funds, $2,765, from the Washington Square residents.

Stanford White, of McKim, Mead & White, *Architect.* Designed both the wood and stucco arch and the marble arch.

Rising at the foot of Fifth Avenue, the white marble triumphal arch (77 ft. H x 30ft. W x 10ft. D) dominates the northern entrance to Washington Square Park. Two winged figures of Victory in relief are carved above the 47-foot-high arch. Emblems of war and peace adorn the columns and a sculpted American Eagle, large decorative stars and 'W's decorate the frieze.

The sculpture on the west pier is *Washington in Peace* with *Justice* and *Wisdom* (inset). The inscribed Latin (*Exitus acta probat*) in the book behind Washington means "The end justifies the deed." The sculpture was created by Alexander Stirling Calder, father of Alexander Calder (the sculptor of mobiles). On the east pier can be found *Washington in War* with *Fame* and *Valor*, by Herman A. MacNeil. Unfortunately, the marble statuary is deteriorating from the city's pollution.

Washington Square Park was constructed in 1827, and soon afterward the area became a wealthy residential area. In 1837, New York University began erecting its first building on the east side of the park. Now, many of the university's buildings are within the park's vicinity.

N.Y.C. Historical District April 29, 1969.

IMMIGRANT RECEIVING STATION

First steps in a new land
ELLIS ISLAND, NEW YORK HARBOR

The original Ellis Island Immigrant Receiving Station opened its doors to the first immigrant, Annie Moore of Cork, Ireland, in 1892. Five years later, it was destroyed by fire. The current building, in the *French Renaissance* style, cost $1.5 million. On December 17, 1900, its first day of operations, 2,251 immigrants were processed. The building remained the nation's primary immigration reception depot until 1924. Only 2 percent of the nearly 17 million or more immigrants who passed through its doors were sent back to their countries of origin. Its peak year was 1907, when 1.2 million immigrants came through Ellis Island. The station closed as an immigration center in 1954. The building has also served as a Coast Guard Station and an enemy-alien detention center.

William A. Boring and **Edward L. Tilton,** *Architects*.

The Immigrant Receiving Station (the principal structure on Ellis Island) is constructed of heavily rusticated limestone and red brick with limestone ornamentation. Between the three colossal arches of the entry are two limestone American Eagle statues (inset). Rising from the four corners of the central pavilion are four 134-foot-high copper-capped towers. Inside, on the second floor, is the building's grandest room, Registry Hall. Its 50-foot vaulted ceiling is adorned with interlocking terra-cotta tiles. Other buildings in this complex include the hospital, powerhouse, dormitories and dining hall. The island itself grew from a sandbar to its current 27-acre size using earth excavated for construction of the New York subway system.

In 1984, the building was closed for renovation and restoration under the direction of Beyer Blinder & Belle/Notter Finegold & Alexander. It was reopened as a National Museum in September 1990.

National Historic Landmark May 11, 1965.

Flatiron Building

Twenty-three skidoo

175 Fifth Avenue at 23rd Street

The Flatiron Building derives its name from its triangular shape created by the intersection of Broadway and Fifth Avenue at 23rd Street. It was the world's tallest building when it was completed in 1902, marking the beginnings of the skyscraper era in New York City.

Daniel H. Burnham of D. H. Burnham & Co., *Architect*. Chicago. Burnham also designed one of the earliest skyscrapers, the Monadnock Building, in Chicago, 1891.

Covering the entire lot, the 21-story, 285-foot-high building extends in an unbroken mass without any setbacks. The steel framework is clad with rusticated limestone and molded terra cotta in the *Renaissance Revival* style. The vertical composition is the classic tripart, based on the divisions of a column (base, shaft and capital top). The base (first four floors) is heavily rusticated, giving the building a solid anchor. The ornate capital, with two-story arches and an enormous cornice, provides a visual stop to the otherwise continuous 12-story shaft.

In the early 1900s, strong down drafts from the building created a spectacle of young ladies' long skirts being lifted, exposing their ankles. Reputedly, their admirers were cleared away with shouts of "Twenty-three skidoo" from the policemen directing traffic.

Originally known as the Fuller Building after its developer, its name changed because of its unusual appearance. Viewed from uptown on Fifth Avenue, the Flatiron Building has been compared to the bow of a ship. Its rounded apex at 23rd Street is only six feet across.

N.Y.C. Landmark September 20, 1966.

MACY★S

The world's largest store

34TH STREET FROM BROADWAY TO SEVENTH AVENUE

As the world's largest store, Macy's boasts more than two million square feet of floor space. Its 300 selling departments stock over a half-million different items. For over 140 years Macy's has served as one of the city's leading retail establishments.

Rowland Hussey Macy, *Nantucket Whaling Captain, Merchant.* Started Macy's in 1858 at Sixth Avenue and 14th Street. The Macy's red star logo was based on a tattoo he had on his hand from his younger days as a Nantucket whaler.

Isidor and **Nathan Straus,** *Merchants.* Originally leasing the rights to the store's glass, china and silver departments, they took controlling interest in Macy's after Rowland Macy's death in 1877 and moved the store to its current location at 34th Street and Broadway in 1902.

De Lemos & Cordes, *Architects.* Designed the original Broadway building.
Robert D. Kohn, *Architect.* Designed the Seventh Avenue addition.

Macy's department store actually consists of two buildings: the Broadway side is the original building and the Seventh Avenue side was added in 1931. The nine-story building (200 ft.W x 700 ft. L) is constructed of red brick and limestone. On the Broadway façade, the middle floors are articulated vertically with superimposed bay windows and four-story high Corinthian columns. Above the bay windows are *Palladian*-style arched windows.

The four caryatids (columns shaped like women) on the 34th Street façade entrance (inset) are by J. Massey Rhind. Other original details on the 34th Street façade include the canopy, clock and turn-of-the century Macy's lettering. By the main entrance, a plaque memorializes the 1912 death of Isidor Straus and his wife in the sinking of the *Titanic*.

The main selling floor has been restored to reveal the 1930s *Art Deco* style.

New York Stock Exchange
The big board
8 Broad Street

Completed in 1903, the New York Stock Exchange houses one of the most important financial institutions in the world.

The **Buttonwood Agreement** (May 17, 1792) is the original document drafted by 24 brokers to form the *New York Stock Exchange Board*. It was named after the buttonwood (sycamore) tree under which their trading of bonds began. A buttonwood tree was planted outside the entrance at 20 Wall Street to commemorate the organization's origins.

George B. Post, *Architect.* Awarded commission for his design.

The *Greek Revival* building has a rusticated two-story base with rectangular and rounded arched openings. Six 52-foot-high Corinthian columns support a classic Greek pediment. Behind the columns, a four-story glass curtain wall admits light into the marble and gilded trading room.

The statuary in the pediment, *Integrity Protecting the Works of Man*, designed by J. Q. A. Ward and Paul Bartlett, includes: *Integrity*, center, *Agriculture* and *Mining* on her left, and *Science*, *Industry* and *Invention* on her right. The original marble statuary was destroyed by pollution and replaced in 1936 by copper and lead figures, which were coated to resemble stone.

The New York Stock Exchange Board has 1,366 members and more than 2,860 U.S. and non-U.S. companies listed on the exchange. The price of a seat fluctuates: in 1817, a seat cost $25; in 1929, $625,000; and ten years later, $85,000. Today, a seat can sell for as much as $2.5 million. In 2000, the average daily trading volume was 1,041.6 million shares, and a record of $43.9 billion was reached. The exchange averaged over one billion shares a day traded for a total of 262.5 billion shares traded during the year 2000.

N.Y.C. Landmark July 9, 1985.

THE MORGAN LIBRARY

Fit for a priceless collection

29 EAST 36TH STREET

This elegant building houses the collection of **Pierpont Morgan** (1837–1913), scion of the powerful financial empire established by Junius Morgan in the mid-1800s. Well known for his gifts to education and the arts, Morgan spared no expense in constructing what has been described as "among [the] most luxuriously appointed private museums in the world." During the stock market crisis of 1907, Pierpont Morgan used his wealth and power to help end the panic and avoid a general financial collapse.

McKim, Mead & White, *Architects.* The 36th Street façade may have been inspired by the Villa Giulia in Rome. The original *Italian Renaissance*-style building, completed in 1906, was constructed of marble blocks laid up without mortar in the manner of classical antiquity. At this time, McKim, Mead & White were the pre-eminent East Coast architects, working in the eclectic classical style espoused by the *École des Beaux Arts* of Paris, the world's foremost school of architecture.

J. P. Morgan, Jr., *Financier and philanthropist.* Morgan's son and heir (1867–1943) opened the Library to the public in 1924 and dedicated it as an institution of research. He built the annex, which contains the present main entrance, in 1928. Under the terms of the gift, the Library will be kept intact until the 100th anniversary of his father's death, in 2013.

The Morgan Library's collection includes prints, rare books and medieval illuminated manuscripts, as well as paintings, drawings and sculpture. Early printed books include William Caxton's *Sarum Hours* (c. 1476). One of the Library's three Gutenberg Bibles is always on display. The palatial East Room, which has an ornate coffered ceiling, murals, and alcoves is filled with portrait medallions and bas-relief figures from antiquity.

N.Y.C. Landmark May 17, 1966. N.Y.C. Interior Landmark March 23, 1982.

Times Square

Crossroads of the world

42ND STREET AT SEVENTH AVENUE AND BROADWAY

Times Square is a triangular area created by the intersection of Seventh Avenue and Broadway at 42nd Street. During the late 1800s, the area was the center for carriage shops and stables, and called Long Acre Square after a similar area in London. In 1904, the square was renamed Times Square in honor of Adolph Ochs' Times Building, home of *The New York Times* daily newspaper. The first theater in the area, the Metropolitan Opera House at Broadway and 40th Street, opened in 1893, and the theater district was born.

"The Great White Way" is a term supposedly coined in 1901 by O. J. Gude, an ad man, for Broadway's glittering electric signs and billboards. In the 1920s, when movie palaces became the rage, the flashing displays reached new heights. Elaborate signboards, including a cascading waterfall, giant cigarette smoke rings and monstrous neon tumbling peanuts, helped create the Times Square visual mystique. By the 1970s, most of the movie palaces had been replaced by glass skyscrapers, and between these office buildings, pornography found a home. Since 1993, the Times Square District has been renovated and rejuvenated to its original status as the city's premiere entertainment center.

The world's first moving electric sign was installed on the Times Building in 1928. The 5-foot-high, 360-foot-long ribbon of 14,800 electric lights displays a message that travels around the building. After several years of darkness, the "motograph" was restored and reilluminated in 1986. It displays up-to-the-minute news flashes from the daily *New York Newsday*.

Times Square's first New Year's Eve celebration, complete with fireworks, took place on December 31, 1904, when *The New York Times* moved its printing presses into the Times Building. It has remained an annual festive tradition, complete with the famous dropping ball.

At the northern end of the square stands a statue of American showman George M. *"Give my regards to Broadway"* Cohan, by George Lober (inset).

PLAZA HOTEL

A grand hotel de luxe

FIFTH AVENUE AND CENTRAL PARK SOUTH (59TH STREET)

This magnificent landmark hotel opened on October 1, 1907. The 18-story, cast-iron, *French Renaissance* building cost a total of $12.5 million to erect and featured 800 rooms, five marble staircases and a two-story ballroom.

Henry J. Hardenbergh, *Architect.* Also designer of the Dakota Apartments.

The hotel's first guest was Alfred G. Vanderbilt, son of Cornelius Vanderbilt, and it has since been host to many famous guests and to society's parties and balls. A portrait of the best known and most troublesome resident—six-year-old Eloise, created by author Kay Thompson—hangs in the lobby.

Its grand vistas, north to Central Park and east to Grand Army Plaza, afford the hotel one of the most prestigious sites in the city. Its exterior consists of a three-story marble base with a ten-story mid-section of white brick, capped by balustraded balconies, a massive cornice and a five-story mansard slate roof with dormers, gables and crest. Two corners are rounded to form towers. Flags flying from the Fifth Avenue façade represent the nations of important foreign guests and dignitaries. The Plaza's insignia, two Ps back to back in a crest, figure in the building's ornamentation. The inset above is a lamp-post detail.

On the first floor are the famous Oak Bar, with its murals of Grand Army Plaza at night, painted by Everett Shinn, and the elegant Palm Court, with its imported Italian caryatids representing the four seasons.

The Plaza has been the quintessential New York hotel for films including *The Great Gatsby, Plaza Suite* and *Author.* In 1907 the Plaza's most expensive room was $25 a night. At this writing, its least expensive room is more than $600 a night. All 60 of the Plaza's suites and its public spaces were elegantly refurbished in 1999–2000.

N.Y.C. Landmark December 9, 1969.

New York Public Library

Reading between the lions

This building is considered one of the finest examples of *Beaux-Arts*-style architecture in America. The library was the result of a merger between the Astor and Lenox Libraries and the Tilden Trust and was constructed on the former Croton Aqueduct Distributing Reservoir. The library opened on May 24, 1911.

John M. Carrère and **Thomas Hastings,** *Architects*. Awarded the commission based upon their competition-winning design.

Dr. John Shaw Billings, *First Director of the Library*. Credited with conceiving the library's basic plan. The Main Reading Room (297 ft. x 78 ft.) was one of Billings's suggestions.

The symmetrical Fifth Avenue façade, constructed of Vermont white marble, sits at the top of a broad flight of steps with expansive terraces on both sides. Three arched bays flanked by paired Corinthian columns form the main entrance. The wings have two-story-high engaged Corinthian columns. Between the columns are arched windows with sculpted lion's mask keystones. A bay with pediments and sculpture completes each end of the building. The building is lavishly ornate, both inside and out with sculpted lions, cherubs and gargoyles. Its 88 miles of bookshelves house over 34 million books, manuscripts, maps and prints. It is considered one of the five great research libraries of the world. Over 11,000 people enter the library on an average day.

The statues of *Beauty* and *Truth* (L-R of the entrance) are by Frederick MacMonnies. Paul Bartlett designed the 11-foot-high figures of (L-R) *History, Drama, Poetry, Religion* and *Romance* on the frieze. The celebrated lions (inset) are by Edward Clark Potter. Their original names were *Lady Astor* and *Lord Lenox*. Mayor La Guardia renamed them *Patience* and *Fortitude*.

National Historical Landmark 1966. N.Y.C. Landmark January 11, 1967.

WOOLWORTH BUILDING

Cathedral of commerce

233 BROADWAY, AT BARCLAY STREET

The Woolworth Building opened on April 24, 1913, when President Wilson pressed a button in Washington, D. C., illuminating its 80,000 lights. The building was the predecessor of the skyscrapers of the 1920s that transformed New York City's skyline. Designed in the *Gothic Revival* style, it took three years to build, and the construction cost of $13.5 million was paid for in cash.

Frank Winfield Woolworth, *Merchant.* After his first five-cent store failed in Utica, N.Y., Woolworth opened a five-and-ten-cent store in Lancaster, Pa., in 1879. Within 32 years, he had established a chain of over 1,000 stores, and the F. W. Woolworth Company flourished for another six decades.

Cass Gilbert, *Architect.* Also designed the U. S. Custom House and U. S. Court House in New York, and the Supreme Court Building in Washington, D. C.

The 60-story building consists of a 30-story base and a 30-story tower capped by a copper-clad pyramidal roof. Rising to a height of 792 feet, the Woolworth Building was the tallest skyscraper for 17 years, until the Bank of Manhattan was completed in 1929. Terra cotta covers the structural steel skeleton from the fourth floor upward. The vertical rows of windows rise between terra-cotta clad piers, emphasizing its verticality. The ornate *Gothic* detailing of cream terra cotta includes flying buttresses, pinnacles, and features sculpted gargoyles, mythical beasts and masks.

The lobby features glass mosaic vaultings, stained-glass ceilings and terra-cotta reliefs. The caricature reliefs of Frank Woolworth counting his nickels and dimes (inset) and Cass Gilbert studying a model of the Woolworth Building were designed by Thomas R. Johnston.

N.Y.C. Landmark April 12, 1983.

GRAND CENTRAL TERMINAL

The noble gateway to New York

42ND STREET AND PARK AVENUE

Designed in the *Beaux-Arts* style, Grand Central Terminal, a multipurpose urban center, was opened to the public in 1913. It was financed by Cornelius Vanderbilt's New York Central Railroad at a cost of $80 million.

Reed & Stem, *Architects.* St. Paul, Minnesota. This competition-winning design team was responsible for the original solutions to the building's functional problems. **Warren & Wetmore,** *Architects.* Responsible for the building's overall design and its *Beaux-Arts* detailing. They also designed the New York Yacht Club.

William J. Wilgus, *Engineer and Vice President of the New York Central Railroad.* Following the electrification of the trains, Wilgus was able to cover the train yards north of the terminal and utilize the air rights for real estate developments.

The terminal's steel frame construction is clad in Stony Creek granite and Bedford limestone. The 42nd Street façade has three grand arches, each framed with colossal Doric columns grouped in pairs. Above the central arch is a 13-foot clock, surrounded by the sculpture of *Mercury, Hercules* and *Minerva* by Jules A. Coutan. Below it is the statue of the founder of the original railroad, Commodore Cornelius Vanderbilt, by Albert De Groot, 1869.

The main concourse (120 ft. W x 275 ft. L x 125 ft. H) is a thoroughfare for half a million passengers a day. Recently restored at a cost of almost $200 million, by **Beyer Blinder Belle,** *Architects,* the terminal was rededicated on September 24, 1998. The marble stonework was restored, chandeliers regilded and the vaulted ceiling's mural, mistakenly painted as a mirrored image by Paul Heleu, returned to its original splendor. A staircase was added to the east end of the main concourse (inset) to match the elaborate west stairs, a double flight of marble steps designed after the grand staircase of the Paris Opera.

N.Y.C. Landmark September 21, 1967.

METROPOLITAN MUSEUM OF ART
The largest art museum in the western hemisphere
FIFTH AVENUE, 80TH STREET TO 83RD STREET

The Metropolitan Museum of Art houses one of the most comprehensive art collections in the world with more than 3 million works of ancient, medieval, classical and modern art. From its *Gothic* origins to its more recent glass-walled additions, the museum reflects the major architectural styles of the last century. Recent additions include the new permanent gallery for the Arts of Korea, which opened on June 9, 1998.

Calvert Vaux and **Jacob Wrey Mould,** *Architects.* Designed the original *Gothic* building, 1874–80, which faced onto Central Park. The arcaded center portion of the west façade is the only visible remnant of the original building.

Richard Morris Hunt, *Architect.* The building's orientation to Fifth Avenue was established in 1895 when R. M. Hunt designed the Fifth Avenue *Beaux-Arts* pavilion and Grand Hall. **Richard Howland Hunt** became *Construction Architect* after his father's death. At the main entrance, three monumental arches are flanked by pairs of Corinthian columns, which support massive blocks of stone. The blocks were intended for sculptures, but monies were never available.

McKim, Mead & White, *Architects.* Designed the restrained *Classical* north and south wings on Fifth Avenue, 1911–13.

Roche, Dinkeloo & Associates, *Architects.* Designed the three glass-walled additions, 1975–82.

Two of the city's landmark buildings have been incorporated into the museum: the façade of the old Assay Office building from Wall Street, built in 1823, is part of the American Wing; and the pediment of the Madison Square Presbyterian Church, 1906, is part of the Museum Library façade.

N.Y.C. Landmark June 9, 1967. Interior Landmark November 15, 1977.

CHRYSLER BUILDING

Dedicated to world commerce and industry

405 LEXINGTON AVENUE AT 42ND STREET

The 77-story *Art Deco*-style building celebrates the automobile as well as the modern skyscraper. In 1930, it became the world's tallest building when architect William Van Alen had the 185-foot spire (assembled secretly in the fire shaft) added to the 925-foot-tall building. The Chrysler Building thus surpassed the just-completed 927-foot-tall Bank of Manhattan (the bank was designed by Van Alen's former partner and rival, H. Craig Severance). Van Alen's record was short-lived, however, as the Empire State Building was completed only a few months later.

Walter P. Chrysler, *Automobile Industrialist.* Founder and president of the Chrysler Automobile Corporation.

William Van Alen, *Architect.*

Constructed of white ceramic brick with stainless steel ornamentation, the Chrysler Building was one of the first to use stainless steel as a building material. The fourth setback (26th floor) is adorned with white and grey brick automobile patterns and is capped at each corner with 10-foot-high winged radiator caps (inset). At the fifth setback, eight stainless steel eaglelike gargoyles perch over the edge.

Although Van Alen's original plan specified lighting this tower of stainless steel arches and triangular windows, it was not illuminated until 1981.

The angular lobby, restored in 1978, consists of multicolored marble and granite; a ceiling mural by Edward Trumball that depicts the Chrysler Building, transportation and industry; and elevator doors and walls, which are decorated with stylized floral designs of exotic inlaid woods.

N.Y.C. Landmark September 12, 1978.

EMPIRE STATE BUILDING

The cathedral of the skies

350 FIFTH AVENUE

The Empire State Building was the world's tallest skyscraper from its completion on May 1, 1931, until 1973, when the former World Trade Center was constructed. Completed in only 18 months, the Empire State Building cost $41 million to build, $19 million under budget.

Shreve, Lamb & Harmon, *Architects.*

John J. Raskob, *Developer.* Conceived of and raised the funding for the Empire State Building at a time when the country was in financial crisis.

Alfred E. Smith, *President of the Empire State Company.* Former Governor of New York State for four terms.

Built on the site of the original Waldorf-Astoria Hotel, the Empire State Building rises 1,454 feet to the top of its T.V. tower. Limestone, granite, nickel, aluminum and over 10 million bricks comprise the exterior. The building's basic components, windows, stone, and steel spandrels were fabricated off site and installed as if on an assembly line. The tower rises from a five-floor base and is capped with a monumental spire. The spire also acts as a lightning conductor and, as a result, the building is struck up to 500 times a year. The three-story-high lobby is finished in European marble, stainless steel and glass that are arranged in geometric patterns typical of the *Art Deco* period.

Immortalized in the 1933 movie *King Kong,* the world-famous building withstood the impact of an off-course B-25 Bomber into the 79th floor in 1945. The top 30 floors were first illuminated in 1977, when the N.Y. Yankees won the World Series. Since then, the tower's colors change to mark various holidays and special events.

N.Y.C. Landmark May 19, 1981. National Historic Landmark October 23, 1986.

ROCKEFELLER CENTER

A city within a city

FIFTH TO SIXTH AVENUES, BETWEEN WEST 48TH & WEST 51ST STREETS

Rockefeller Center is the world's largest privately owned business and entertainment complex. The original complex of 14 buildings on 12 acres of land was the first development where skyscrapers were designed as a group. Initially, the site was to provide a home for New York's Metropolitan Opera House. In 1929, after the stock market crash, the Metropolitan Opera withdrew from the project, and, in order to avoid financial disaster, the focus of the complex shifted to a mixed business center. The *Art Deco* complex, built between 1931 and 1939, replaced more than 200 smaller buildings in the area and employed more than 225,000 people during the Depression.

John D. Rockefeller, Jr., *Developer.*

Hood, Godley & Fouilhoux; Corbett, Harrison & MacMurray; Reinhard & Hofmeister, *Architects.* These firms worked together to design the first architecturally coordinated complex in New York City.

The centerpiece of the complex is the GE Building at 30 Rockefeller Plaza (formerly the RCA Building). The slender limestone tower rises from a four-foot granite base to a height of 850 feet. Its vertical rows of windows soar between limestone with aluminum trim for 70 stories. It is this combination of high and low buildings with gardens and plazas that creates the grandeur and spaciousness of Rockefeller Center.

More than 100 murals, mosaics and sculptures, by 39 different artists, adorn Rockefeller Center. Two of the best known are *Prometheus*, in the Sunken Garden, and *Atlas* (inset) in front of the International Building.

The center is also the home of Radio City Music Hall, the Rainbow Room and NBC Studios. Over the years, Rockefeller Center has expanded to incorporate 19 buildings on 22 acres.

N.Y.C. Landmark April 23, 1985. National Historic Landmark 1987.

Radio City Music Hall

Showplace of the nation
1260 Avenue of the Americas

When Radio City Music Hall opened as a vaudeville entertainment house on December 27, 1932, it was the nation's largest theater. The *Art Deco* styling combined with the palatial interior space celebrates a high point in American theater design.

Samuel L. "Roxy" Rothafel, *First Director of the Music Hall.* Famous for his combination of silent movies and live entertainment, Roxy was responsible for the hall's design and entertainment policies.

Donald Deskey, *Interior Designer.* Won the commission with his strikingly stylized *Art Deco* theater design.

The grand foyer (60 ft. H x 60 ft. W) is an entire city block long. It is graced with floor-to-ceiling mirrors and drapes, two 29-foot-long chandeliers and a 24-carat gold leaf ceiling. *The Fountain of Youth* mural by Ezra Winter is the backdrop for the foyer's grand staircase. The 5,874-seat auditorium is dominated by the golden proscenium arches radiating from the stage. Roxy's analogy was that of the sun setting on the ocean. The 144-foot-wide stage has a 43-foot diameter turntable and three cross-sections that can be lowered or raised independently. The stage's hydraulic system was so innovative that the Navy studied it for its applications to aircraft carrier technology.

The world-renowned precision dancers *The Rockettes* moved to the music hall from the Roxy Theater in 1934. The troupe began in St. Louis in 1925 as the *Sixteen Missouri Rockets* under the direction of Russell Markert. With a company of 60 dancers, 36 perform on stage at a given time.

The hall has been the venue for premiere film showings, live stage productions, concerts, television events, the Moscow Circus, the Grammy Awards and the famous annual Christmas Spectacular. In 1979, the music hall's interior was restored to its original 1930s design.

N.Y.C. Interior Landmark March 28, 1978. N.Y.C. Landmark April 23, 1985.

UNITED NATIONS

Promoting international peace and security

FIRST AVENUE, FROM 42ND STREET TO 48TH STREET

The United Nations complex of three buildings—Secretariat, General Assembly and Conference Building—was designed by an international committee of 14 architects. Its 18-acre site was purchased with a gift of $8.5 million from John D. Rockefeller, Jr. Built from 1947 to 1953, the cost of the three buildings was approximately $67 million.

Le Corbusier (Charles-Édouard Jeanneret), *Design Architect.* France (born Switzerland). Credited with the conceptual design for the complex.

Wallace K. Harrison, Harrison & Abramovitz, *Architectural Chairman and Construction Architect.* Also the Director of the Board of Architects for the Lincoln Center.

Trygve Halvdan Lie, *First Secretary General of the United Nations, 1946–53.*

The name "United Nations" was coined by President Franklin D. Roosevelt in 1941 to describe the countries allied against the Axis Powers in World War II. The name replaced the "League of Nations" that had been established by the peace treaties of World War I. In 1945, the UN Charter establishing the United Nations was drafted by its original 51 member countries. There are now some 180 nations represented.

The Secretariat is the 39-story, 544-foot-tall, narrow vertical building. Completed in 1950, it was New York's first building with an all-glass curtain wall: green glass set in an aluminum grid rises unbroken to the roofline. Its north and south elevations, 72-feet wide, are covered in Vermont white marble. The General Assembly is the sculptured limestone building with concave roof and central dome. The Conference Building, facing the East River, links the Secretariat with the General Assembly.

Solomon R. Guggenheim Museum

Let each man exercise the art he knows

1071 Fifth Avenue

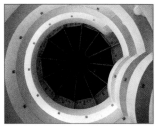

The Guggenheim Museum is one of the city's most unique and controversial buildings. After 16 years of design and construction changes to accommodate the city's Department of Building Codes, the museum's directors and public outcry, the museum opened in October 1959. The building's "organic" spiral form is completely foreign to the traditional Fifth Avenue façade of aligned rectangular buildings facing Central Park.

Solomon R. Guggenheim, *Copper Magnate.* Established the Solomon R. Guggenheim Foundation for his collection of non-objective art.

Baroness Hilla Rebay, *First Director of the Museum.* Under her guidance Guggenheim's collection shifted from the Old Masters to abstract art. She was instrumental in creating both the collection and the museum, and in commissioning Frank Lloyd Wright to design the building.

Frank Lloyd Wright, *Architect.* A paramount force in modern architecture and design. The Guggenheim is his only building in New York City.

Completion of the project was facilitated by the efforts of **Harry Guggenheim,** president of the foundation after Solomon R. Guggenheim's death in 1949, and **James J. Sweeney**, the museum's second director.

The museum is constructed of cream-colored reinforced concrete. The main gallery—an expanding spiral—is attached to the administration building— a smaller circular structure—by a concrete slab. The art is displayed along a quarter-mile-long ramp that spirals 92-feet up to a domed skylight. The permanent art collection housed in small galleries off the ramp includes works by Paul Klee, Wassily Kandinsky, Marc Chagall, Robert Delaunay and Fernand Léger. Wright intended natural lighting from the glazing that rings the outer wall and from the skylight. Alterations were made during the 1980s, but the main gallery has since been restored to Wright's original design.

N.Y.C. Landmark August 14, 1990.

LINCOLN CENTER

For the performing arts

COLUMBUS AVENUE TO AMSTERDAM AVENUE, 62ND STREET TO 66TH STREET

Lincoln Center, a 14-acre complex of buildings that cost a total of $185 million to construct, is dedicated to drama, music and dance. Although Lincoln Center was criticized from the beginning by urban planners and by architects alike, it remains the largest, most comprehensive performing arts center in New York City. It caters to an annual audience of 5.5 million and supports a staff of more than 6,800.

Robert Moses, *New York City's Slum Clearance Administrator.* He proposed turning the area (formerly aging row houses) into a cultural venue.

John D. Rockefeller, III, *Head of the Building Committee.*

Wallace K. Harrison, *Director of the Board of Architects.* Also a member of the architectural board for the United Nations and Rockefeller Center.

Surrounding an elevated plaza, the buildings are rectangular in plan, with flat roofs and colonnades, and finished in white travertine marble. Their *Classical* style and layout is often compared to that of an ancient acropolis.

The three principal buildings are: The **Metropolitan Opera House,** 1966, **Wallace K. Harrison** of Harrison & Abramovitz, *Architect.* Facing Broadway at the center of the plaza, the Opera House dominates the complex. Behind its 10-story-high arched glass walls are a vista of plush red carpets, sweeping marble stairs and a gold leaf ceiling. In the lobby are two large murals by Marc Chagall; The **New York State Theater,** 1964, **Philip C. Johnson** and **Richard Foster,** *Architects.* Located on the south side of the plaza, the New York State Theater is the home of the New York City Opera and Ballet; and **Avery Fisher Hall,** 1962, **Max Abramovitz** of Harrison & Abramovitz, *Architect.* Housing the New York Philharmonic, Avery Fisher Hall stands on the north side. In an effort to improve the acoustics, the concert hall has been renovated several times. Other buildings in the complex include the Vivian Beaumont Theater, 1965; the Library and Museum of the Performing Arts, 1965; the Juilliard School of Music, 1968; and the Guggenheim Band Shell, 1969.

WORLD TRADE CENTER

DECEMBER 1970 – SEPTEMBER 11, 2001

CHURCH STREET, BETWEEN LIBERTY STREET AND VESEY STREET

"Terrorist attacks can shake the foundations of our biggest buildings, but they cannot touch the foundation of America. These acts shattered steel, but they cannot dent the steel of American resolve."
—PRESIDENT GEORGE W. BUSH, SEPTEMBER 12, 2001

"The catastrophe that turned the foot of Manhattan into the mouth of Hell…"
—HENDRIK HERTZBERG, *The New Yorker*, SEPTEMBER 24, 2001

On the crystal-clear morning of September 11, 2001, New York's and America's most shattering peacetime tragedy reverberated around the world. Two hijacked jetliners struck the North (8:48 AM) and South (9:04 AM) Towers of the World Trade Center in rapid succession, exploding into black clouds of smoke, raging flames, and a hailstorm of fiery debris. Within two hours, the 110-story Twin Towers collapsed into a mass of twisted steel, rubble and dust.

An estimated 2,831 people have died, or are missing and presumed dead, including 416 heroic emergency/rescue personnel, and 147 passengers and crew on the two hijacked planes. The terrorist attack claimed more lives than the surprise bombing of Pearl Harbor, Hawaii (2,388), which brought the United States into World War II on December 7, 1941.

The world's largest commercial complex was created to facilitate the ever-growing interdependence of the world community. Some 50,000 people from dozens of nations had worked at the center and more than 1.8 million visitors a year toured the 16-acre complex. Located in the Financial District, the center was designed by *Architect* **Minoru Yamasaki** for the **Port Authority of New York and New Jersey. Emery Roth & Sons** were the *Construction Architects* for the project, which was more than 10 years in the building, on landfill reclaimed from the Hudson River. Its cost was estimated at $700 million.

The World Trade Center was first targeted by terrorists on February 26, 1993, when an explosion in the underground parking garage killed six people and injured more than 1,000.

Future plans for the site, which will include a memorial to the victims of 9/11, are under debate by the city and a nation still in shock over the cataclysm.

BIBLIOGRAPHY

A FEW OF THE MAJOR SOURCES USED FOR RESEARCHING THE ARCHITECTURE AND HISTORY OF NEW YORK CITY

The Landmarks of New York
Barbaralee Diamonstein

Blue Guide New York
Carol von Pressentin Wright

The Architecture of New York City
Donald Martin Reynolds

The WPA Guide to New York City
Federal Writers Project, 1930

New York 1900
R. A. Stern, G. Gilmartin, J. Massengale

New York 1930
R. A. Stern, G. Gilmartin, T. Mellins

The Skyscraper
Paul Goldberger

AIA Guide to New York City
Elliot Willensky & Norval White

New York, A Guide to the Metropolis
Gerard R. Wolfe

History Preserved, A Guide to New York City Landmarks and Historic Districts
Harmon Goldstone & Martha Dalrymple

This edition published by DOVETAIL BOOKS.

2002 DOVETAIL BOOKS

ISBN 0-9636673-0-0

Printed and bound in China

20 19 18 17 16 15 14 13 12 11 10 9 8